IN ASSOCIATION WITH

✕SQA

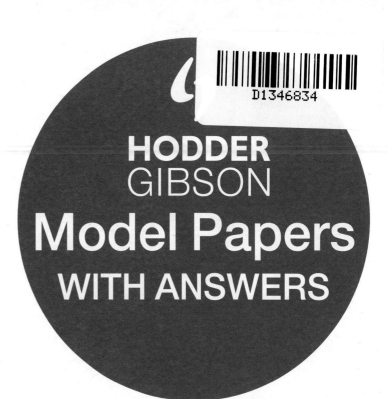

D1346834

HODDER GIBSON
Model Papers
WITH ANSWERS

PLUS: Official SQA 2014 & 2015
Past Papers With Answers

National 5
Graphic Communication

Model Papers, 2014 & 2015 Exams

HODDER
GIBSON
AN HACHETTE UK COMPANY

This book contains the official SQA 2014 and 2015 Exams for National 5 Graphic Communication, with associated SQA answers.

In addition the book contains model papers, together with answers, plus study skills advice. These papers, some of which may include a limited number of previously published SQA questions, have been specially commissioned by Hodder Gibson, and have been written by experienced senior teachers and examiners in line with the new National 5 syllabus and assessment outlines, Spring 2013. This is not SQA material but has been devised to provide further practice for National 5 examinations in 2014 and beyond.

Hodder Gibson is grateful to the copyright holders, as credited on the final page of the Answer Section, for permission to use their material. Every effort has been made to trace the copyright holders and to obtain their permission for the use of copyright material. Hodder Gibson will be happy to receive information allowing us to rectify any error or omission in future editions.

Hachette UK's policy is to use papers that are natural, renewable and recyclable products and made from wood grown in sustainable forests. The logging and manufacturing processes are expected to conform to the environmental regulations of the country of origin.

Orders: please contact Bookpoint Ltd, 130 Park Drive, Milton Park, Abingdon, Oxon OX14 4SE. Telephone: (44) 01235 827720. Fax: (44) 01235 400454. Lines are open 9.00–5.00, Monday to Saturday, with a 24-hour message answering service. Visit our website at www.hoddereducation.co.uk. Hodder Gibson can be contacted direct on: Tel: 0141 848 1609; Fax: 0141 889 6315; email: hoddergibson@hodder.co.uk

This collection first published in 2015 by
Hodder Gibson, an imprint of Hodder Education,
An Hachette UK Company
2a Christie Street
Paisley PA1 1NB

Typeset by Aptara, Inc.

Printed in the UK

A catalogue record for this title is available from the British Library

ISBN: 978-1-4718-6060-7

3 2 1

2016 2015

Introduction

Study Skills – what you need to know to pass exams!

Pause for thought

Many students might skip quickly through a page like this. After all, we all know how to revise. Do you really though?

Think about this:

"IF YOU ALWAYS DO WHAT YOU ALWAYS DO, YOU WILL ALWAYS GET WHAT YOU HAVE ALWAYS GOT."

Do you like the grades you get? Do you want to do better? If you get full marks in your assessment, then that's great! Change nothing! This section is just to help you get that little bit better than you already are.

There are two main parts to the advice on offer here. The first part highlights fairly obvious things but which are also very important. The second part makes suggestions about revision that you might not have thought about but which WILL help you.

Part 1

DOH! It's so obvious but …

Start revising in good time

Don't leave it until the last minute – this will make you panic.

Make a revision timetable that sets out work time AND play time.

Sleep and eat!

Obvious really, and very helpful. Avoid arguments or stressful things too – even games that wind you up. You need to be fit, awake and focused!

Know your place!

Make sure you know exactly **WHEN and WHERE** your exams are.

Know your enemy!

Make sure you know what to expect in the exam.

How is the paper structured?

How much time is there for each question?

What types of question are involved?

Which topics seem to come up time and time again?

Which topics are your strongest and which are your weakest?

Are all topics compulsory or are there choices?

Learn by DOING!

There is no substitute for past papers and practice papers – they are simply essential! Tackling this collection of papers and answers is exactly the right thing to be doing as your exams approach.

Part 2

People learn in different ways. Some like low light, some bright. Some like early morning, some like evening / night. Some prefer warm, some prefer cold. But everyone uses their BRAIN and the brain works when it is active. Passive learning – sitting gazing at notes – is the most INEFFICIENT way to learn anything. Below you will find tips and ideas for making your revision more effective and maybe even more enjoyable. What follows gets your brain active, and active learning works!

Activity 1 – Stop and review

Step 1

When you have done no more than 5 minutes of revision reading STOP!

Step 2

Write a heading in your own words which sums up the topic you have been revising.

Step 3

Write a summary of what you have revised in no more than two sentences. Don't fool yourself by saying, "I know it, but I cannot put it into words". That just means you don't know it well enough. If you cannot write your summary, revise that section again, knowing that you must write a summary at the end of it. Many of you will have notebooks full of blue/black ink writing. Many of the pages will not be especially attractive or memorable so try to liven them up a bit with colour as you are reviewing and rewriting. **This is a great memory aid, and memory is the most important thing.**

Activity 2 – Use technology!

Why should everything be written down? Have you thought about "mental" maps, diagrams, cartoons and colour to help you learn? And rather than write down notes, why not record your revision material?

What about having a text message revision session with friends? Keep in touch with them to find out how and what they are revising and share ideas and questions.

Why not make a video diary where you tell the camera what you are doing, what you think you have learned and what you still have to do? No one has to see or hear it, but the process of having to organise your thoughts in a formal way to explain something is a very important learning practice.

Be sure to make use of electronic files. You could begin to summarise your class notes. Your typing might be slow, but it will get faster and the typed notes will be easier to read than the scribbles in your class notes. Try to add different fonts and colours to make your work stand out. You can easily Google relevant pictures, cartoons and diagrams which you can copy and paste to make your work more attractive and **MEMORABLE**.

Activity 3 – This is it. Do this and you will know lots!

Step 1

In this task you must be very honest with yourself! Find the SQA syllabus for your subject (www.sqa.org.uk). Look at how it is broken down into main topics called MANDATORY knowledge. That means stuff you MUST know.

Step 2

BEFORE you do ANY revision on this topic, write a list of everything that you already know about the subject. It might be quite a long list but you only need to write it once. It shows you all the information that is already in your long-term memory so you know what parts you do not need to revise!

Step 3

Pick a chapter or section from your book or revision notes. Choose a fairly large section or a whole chapter to get the most out of this activity.

With a buddy, use Skype, Facetime, Twitter or any other communication you have, to play the game "If this is the answer, what is the question?". For example, if you are revising Geography and the answer you provide is "meander", your buddy would have to make up a question like "What is the word that describes a feature of a river where it flows slowly and bends often from side to side?".

Make up 10 "answers" based on the content of the chapter or section you are using. Give this to your buddy to solve while you solve theirs.

Step 4

Construct a wordsearch of at least 10 × 10 squares. You can make it as big as you like but keep it realistic. Work together with a group of friends. Many apps allow you to make wordsearch puzzles online. The words and phrases can go in any direction and phrases can be split. Your puzzle must only contain facts linked to the topic you are revising. Your task is to find 10 bits of information to hide in your puzzle, but you must not repeat information that you used in Step 3. DO NOT show where the words are. Fill up empty squares with random letters. Remember to keep a note of where your answers are hidden but do not show your friends. When you have a complete puzzle, exchange it with a friend to solve each other's puzzle.

Step 5

Now make up 10 questions (not "answers" this time) based on the same chapter used in the previous two tasks. Again, you must find NEW information that you have not yet used. Now it's getting hard to find that new information! Again, give your questions to a friend to answer.

Step 6

As you have been doing the puzzles, your brain has been actively searching for new information. Now write a NEW LIST that contains only the new information you have discovered when doing the puzzles. Your new list is the one to look at repeatedly for short bursts over the next few days. Try to remember more and more of it without looking at it. After a few days, you should be able to add words from your second list to your first list as you increase the information in your long-term memory.

FINALLY! Be inspired...

Make a list of different revision ideas and beside each one write **THINGS I HAVE** tried, **THINGS I WILL** try and **THINGS I MIGHT** try. Don't be scared of trying something new.

And remember – "FAIL TO PREPARE AND PREPARE TO FAIL!"

National 5 Graphic Communication

The course

The aims of the course are to enable you to understand how graphic communication is used every day in design, industry and society and to ensure you learn skills and techniques to create graphics to suit any number of purposes.

The types of graphics you will be able to create include:

- **preliminary** design graphics
- technical **production** drawings
- high-impact **promotional** and information graphics.

These are known as the **3 Ps**.

All of your coursework projects and exam questions are based on these types of graphics. The knowledge you need for the exam will come from the work you do during your project work in class.

How you are assessed and graded

The grade you achieve at the end of your course depends on a number of assessments.

Unit Assessment

Both units (2D Graphic Communication and 3D & Pictorial Graphic Communication) are assessed on a pass or fail basis. You must pass both units in order to qualify for a course award.

Course Assessment

Your grade for the National 5 course is derived from two course assessments:

- **The assignment:** this is the project you will complete during the second half of your course. It is worth 60 marks.
- **The course exam paper:** this is the exam you will sit at the end of the course. It is worth 60 marks.

Your marks for the two assessments are added together to give you a total out of 120 marks.

The exam

Duration: 1 hour and 30 minutes

Marks available: 60

The exam will include a mix of short and more extended response questions about the graphics required to design, produce or promote a product.

You should look at the marks awarded for each question. This is a good indicator of the length of answer you should give. For example, for a 3-mark question you will need to make three distinct points, while for a 1-mark question you will need to make only a single point. You should allow yourself around one and a half minutes per mark.

Sketching

Exam questions will be set so that you can answer in writing. However, some questions will invite you to answer using annotated sketches or drawings and space will be left so that you can sketch your answer. **Always take this opportunity.**

Remember:

- This is an exam about graphics and you have all the graphic skills you need.
- It is easier and quicker to describe your answer graphically with annotations than it is to write about it.
- The quality of sketching will not be assessed but the clarity of your answer is important. So make sure your sketches and annotations are clear.

Skills and knowledge

The exam will test you on the following skills and knowledge:

- **Problem solving:** How would you model, render or assemble a 3D CAD model?
- **Creative skills:** How has the graphic designer used design elements and principles to achieve an effective layout?
- **DTP features and edits:** How has the graphic designer used DTP (desktop publishing) software to achieve an effective layout?
- **Advantages and disadvantages:** What are the best methods to choose when creating graphics?
- **Knowledge of drawing standards:** What drawing standards should be applied to orthographic and pictorial drawings?
- **Spatial awareness:** Can you interpret and understand drawings?
- **Graphics in society:** How do graphics affect society? How do we use information graphics?
- **Graphics and the environment:** How can we create and use graphics without damaging our fragile environment?

Using this book

Practising the type of questions you are likely to face in the National 5 exam is vital if you are to achieve your highest possible grade. This book will give you experience of the problem solving and creative layout questions you will encounter in the exam.

Answering 3D CAD modelling problem solving questions

You should always:

- study the model
- identify what modelling techniques have been used (extrude or revolve)
- describe the steps: new sketch, draw profile, select axis, revolve, etc.
- include the dimensions provided
- describe any additional edits used: array, subtract, shell, etc.
- and, importantly, make annotated sketches to show the steps clearly.

Answering creative layout questions

These questions will ask you to identify how DTP features have been used in a layout and how design elements and principles have been used. Some questions will test your knowledge further by asking you to explain how the use of these features improves the layout.

You should always:

- study the layout (don't rush this!)
- identify the DTP feature(s) and design elements and principles used.
  - Think carefully about how they improve the layout: do they add contrast, create harmony, suggest depth, develop a dominant focal point, unify the layout, create emphasis, change the balance or connect or separate parts? The feature you are asked about will do one of these things. Your task is to identify what it does and explain how it does it.

At the end of the exam, don't forget to read over your answers. Read the questions again and double-check that you have answered the question that was asked. You should have plenty of time.

Good luck!

Remember that the rewards for passing National 5 Graphic Communication are well worth it! Your pass will help you get the future you want for yourself. In the exam, be confident in your own ability. If you're not sure how to answer a question, trust your instincts and just give it a go anyway. Keep calm and don't panic! GOOD LUCK!

Oh, and there is a really exciting Higher course waiting for you next year; we'll see you there!

Model Paper 1

Whilst this Model Paper has been specially commissioned by Hodder Gibson for use as practice for the National 5 exams, the key reference documents remain the SQA Specimen Paper 2013 and the SQA Past Papers 2014 and 2015.

National Qualifications
MODEL PAPER 1

Graphic Communication

Duration — 1 hour and 30 minutes

Total marks — 60

Attempt ALL questions.

All dimensions are in mm.

All technical sketches and drawings use third angle projection.

You may use rulers, compasses or trammels for measuring.

Use **blue** or **black** ink.

Before leaving the examination room you must give this booklet to the Invigilator.
If you do not, you may lose all the marks for this paper.

HODDER GIBSON
GIBSON
LEARN MORE

MARKS | DO NOT WRITE IN THIS MARGIN

1. Cheetah Dynamics, a sports equipment company, is marketing a new range of sports shoes. The mini-ad they have produced will be used in sports magazines. The colours in the layout were chosen carefully. The red company name stands out well.

(a) State why using the colour red helps the company name to stand out against the blue and white background.   1

_____

_____

The designer wanted to create unity by making connections between different items in the layout.

(b) State the DTP feature that allows the body text to follow the shape of the sprinter.   1

_____

When line is used in a layout it can have several functions.

(c) Explain the function of the lines in this layout.   1

_____

_____

MARKS | DO NOT WRITE IN THIS MARGIN

1. **(continued)**

(d) State the name of the DTP feature that produced the **waves in the slogan** above the sports shoes.　1

_____

(e) State the name of the other DTP feature used on the **wavy text**.　1

_____

(f) Explain how shaping the wavy text in this way improves the layout.　1

_____

_____

The blue background **colour fill** was created by the designer.

(g) State the name of the fill effect used in the blue background.　1

_____

Total marks　7

MARKS | DO NOT WRITE IN THIS MARGIN

2. A furniture designer has created some preliminary sketches for a new chair. These sketches were given to a CAD technician who will make a 3D CAD model.

Plan

Elevation

End Elevation

Chair arm

1000

Ø 80

Pictorial View

The CAD technician used the revolve command to model the arms of the chair.

(a) Describe, **using the correct dimensions and 3D CAD modelling terms**, how you would use 3D CAD software to model one arm of the chair. **Do not model the slots in the arm.** You may use sketches to support your answer.

3

_____

_____

_____

MARKS | DO NOT WRITE IN THIS MARGIN

2.   (continued)

The chair requires two arms – one for the left and one for the right. The CAD technician modelled the left-hand arm first.

(b) Describe how the CAD technician can make an identical right-hand arm without starting a new model.   **2**

_____

_____

_____

The chair has four parts, made from three components:

*   the left-hand arm

*   the right-hand arm

*   the seat/back component (used twice).

(continued overleaf)

MARKS

2. (continued)

(c) Describe the CAD constraints used to make a CAD assembly of the four parts. Use sketches to illustrate your answer.   **4**

_____

_____

_____

_____

_____

2. (continued)

Total marks   9

3. CAD production drawings for the manufacture of a plastic fixing clip are shown below.

    The drawings were to be produced in accordance with British Standards conventions but they are not correct.

    To enable the manufacture of the clip, the production drawings require one more dimension, dimension 'X'.

    (a) Identify this missing dimension and add it to an orthographic view. There is no need to add the size, just show the leader and dimension lines and put an 'X' in place of the size. Apply the correct drawing standards.   **2**

MARKS

3. (continued)

(b) Identify eight British Standards drawing **errors** or **omissions** on the orthographic production drawings on *Page seven*. Circle and number each error on the drawing and describe each error in the table below. An example has been given.

8

Table of British Standards errors and omissions in the fixing clip production drawing	
Your numbered error or omission	Description of error or omission
1	This should be a centre line, not a solid line.

The clip drawings were produced using 3D CAD modelling software. The plastic clip will be used inside a flatscreen TV which is being designed and assembled in Scotland.

All of the components are made in a factory in China before being shipped over to Scotland.

(c) Describe two ways in which **CAD models** and **drawing standards** can make this **international work** easier.

CAD Models:

1

_____

_____

Drawing Standards:

1

_____

_____

MARKS

3. (continued)

The company is always trying to improve component design. To help their designers they are transferring all of their drawings and design work from manual drawing boards to 3D CAD models.

(d) Explain two ways in which this change will benefit the designer.

2

The plastic clip is assembled with two other components. The drawings below show the orthographic exploded views of all three components.

(continued overleaf)

MARKS | DO NOT WRITE IN THIS MARGIN

3.   (continued)

The exploded pictorial drawings below represent the clip assembly.

Five of them are incorrect and one is correct.

(e) Identify the exploded pictorial view that matches the clip assembly on the previous page.

Exploded pictorial view _____ matches the clip assembly on the previous page.

1

Total marks 15

MARKS

4. A hospital has employed a graphic designer to improve the layout of signs and notices for patients.

The original sign and the improved sign are shown below.

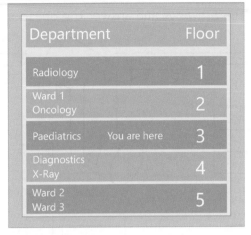

Original sign   **Improved sign**

Colour was an important consideration when designing the improved sign.

(a) Explain how the new colours improved the sign.   2

_____

_____

_____

A survey of patients and visitors preferred the choice of typeface (font) in the improved sign.

(b) Suggest a reason why the new typeface was preferred.   1

_____

_____

Visitors felt that it was easier and quicker to understand the improved sign.

(c) Identify two layout features, excluding typeface, that make the improved sign quicker to understand.   2

_____

_____

_____

Total marks   5

MARKS | DO NOT WRITE IN THIS MARGIN

5. A range of production drawings for a domestic wall hook are shown. The hook comprises two components, the hook and the wall bracket, plus a standard component fixing screw.

Study the drawings and answer the questions.

(a) State which of the two isometric exploded views is **incorrectly** exploded.

Isometric exploded view _____ is incorrectly exploded.   1

(b) Explain why this view is **incorrectly** exploded.   1

_____

_____

_____

_____

The fixing screw is missing from the exploded views.

VIEW A   **VIEW B**

Isometric exploded views

(c) Indicate the position and direction of the fixing screw on the correctly exploded isometric view.   1

5.   (continued)

Wall hook assembly drawings

ELEVATION   END ELEVATION   HOOK ASSEMBLY

(d)   Identify the sectional view below that matches section A–A above.

Section A–A is view _____.   1

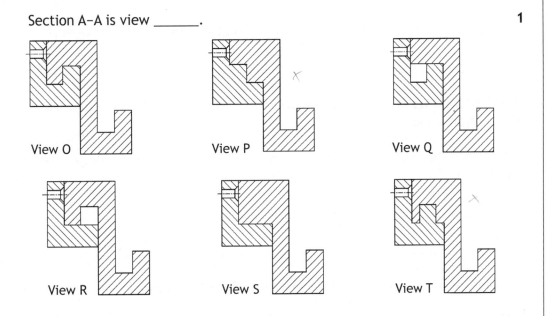

View O   View P   View Q

View R   View S   View T

(e)   Identify the sectional plan view below that matches section B–B above.

Section B–B is view _____.   1

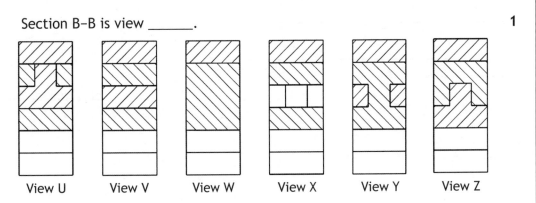

View U   View V   View W   View X   View Y   View Z

MARKS

5.   **(continued)**

Exploded views and sectional views are commonly used in production drawings.

(f)   Describe one benefit that **exploded views** provide.   1

_____

_____

(g)   Describe one benefit that **sectional views** provide. Do not repeat an answer from (f).   1

_____

_____

In sectional drawings there are features that should not be sectioned or cross-hatched.

(h)   Name one common feature or component that should **not** be sectioned.   1

_____

Production drawings can be shown in two main types: assembly drawings and component drawings.

(i)   Describe the difference between assembly drawings and component drawings.   1

_____

_____

Component drawings are dimensioned to support manufacture.

(j)   State why dimensions are added to component drawings and not to assembly drawings.   1

_____

_____

Total marks 10

MARKS | DO NOT WRITE IN THIS MARGIN

6. The four main types of information graphs and charts are shown below.

Pie chart

Bar graph

Line graph

Average Holiday Prices (in £)			
	Britain	Europe	America
Spring	1800	1600	2100
Summer	2200	2000	2400
Autumn	1700	1600	1900
Winter	1350	1300	1650

Table

Two different sets of statistics are shown below.

Each of the statistics can be made more visual by creating an information graph or chart to display the figures.

Statistics A
Annual ice cream sales

January	950 ltr
February	800 ltr
March	1250 ltr
April	3100 ltr
May	2750 ltr
June	4500 ltr
July	5600 ltr
August	6200 ltr
September	4210 ltr
October	1220 ltr
November	1000 ltr
December	1400 ltr

Statistics B
Road bike technical data
Model

Roadster — Wheel size **590cm** Frame size **147cm** Gears **9** Weight **13kg**

Flyer — Wheel size **602cm** Frame size **152cm** Gears **12** Weight **12kg**

Kingfisher — Wheel size **600cm** Frame size **155cm** Gears **9** Weight **14kg**

Draper — Wheel size **588cm** Frame size **148cm** Gears **8** Weight **14kg**

XRB — Wheel size **640cm** Frame size **160cm** Gears **10** Weight **12kg**

Speedster — Wheel size **580cm** Frame size **154cm** Gears **9** Weight **15kg**

(a) State the best type of information graphic to show the trends over the year in **Statistics A**.   1

_____

(b) Explain why this is the best type of graph or chart to display **Statistics A**.   1

_____

_____

(c) State the best type of information graphic to display the data in **Statistics B**.   1

_____

(d) Explain why this is the best type of graph or chart to display **Statistics B**.   1

_____

_____

Total marks   4

MARKS

7. An architecture company makes use of preliminary, production and promotional graphics.

FLOOR PLAN v1.0	
HOUSE NAME:	THE ROCKWELL
SCALE:	
UNITS ARE IN M	
IF IN DOUBT, ASK!	
DRAWN BY:	CLARE HALLIDAY
APPROVED BY:	JOE MASON
DATE:	8TH JULY

To enable the builder to start constructing the house, more information needs to be added to the floor plan.

(a) State three key items of information missing from the floor plan.   3

_____

_____

_____

(b) Add the symbol for a radiator to any one of the rooms.   1

Total marks   4

MARKS

8. A poster designed by a graphic artist to encourage young people to consider university courses is shown.

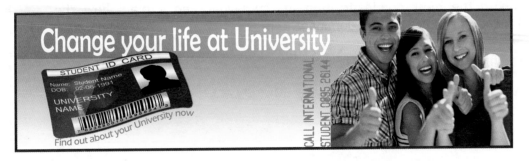

(a) Describe how the graphic artist created unity in the layout.   **1**

_____

_____

(b) Describe how the graphic artist created depth in the layout.   **1**

_____

_____

The graphic artist worked hard to design an organised layout. This was achieved by using alignment.

(c) Describe where alignment occurs in the layout.   **1**

_____

_____

The designer used colour to create contrast in the layout.

(d) Describe one other way in which contrast has been created in this layout.   **1**

_____

_____

The layout is to be used on the side of double-decker buses in towns around the country.

(e) Explain why contrast is important in a promotional layout like this one.   **1**

_____

_____

MARKS

8.   (continued)

(f) Choose the most dominant item in the layout and explain how the designer made it the most dominant item.   1

The most dominant item is_____

The designer created dominance by_____

_____

_____

Total marks   6

[END OF MODEL PAPER]

Model Paper 2

Whilst this Model Paper has been specially commissioned by Hodder Gibson for use as practice for the National 5 exams, the key reference documents remain the SQA Specimen Paper 2013 and the SQA Past Papers 2014 and 2015.

HODDER
GIBSON
LEARN MORE

National Qualifications
MODEL PAPER 2

Graphic Communication

Duration — 1 hour and 30 minutes

Total marks — 60

Attempt ALL questions.

All dimensions are in mm.

All technical sketches and drawings use third angle projection.

You may use rulers, compasses or trammels for measuring.

Use **blue** or **black** ink.

Before leaving the examination room you must give this booklet to the Invigilator.
If you do not, you may lose all the marks for this paper.

MARKS | DO NOT WRITE IN THIS MARGIN

1. Zeus Electronics are promoting their new communicator, the L-COM. Their promotions team have drawn up two promotional layouts for consideration, shown below.

L-COM Promotional layout 1

L-COM Promotional layout 2

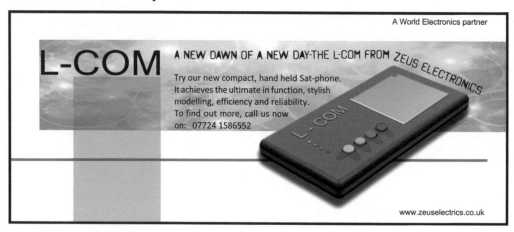

Layout 1 was produced first. DTP edits were then made to some of the items to create layout 2.

(a) State the names of the DTP edits used to change the following items between layout 1 and layout 2.   4

The L-COM product name

DTP edit _____

The slogan ('A NEW DAWN ...' etc.)

DTP edit _____

The body text

DTP edit _____

The image of the L-COM product

DTP edit _____

MARKS

1. **(continued)**

   It is important to create unity in a layout in order to hold the layout together and improve visual impact.

   (b) Describe two ways in which the graphic designer has created unity in layout 2.

   2

   _____

   _____

   _____

   In both layouts the product image of the L-COM communicator is the dominant item in the layout.

   (c) Explain two things the graphic designer has done to make the product image the dominant item.

   2

   _____

   _____

   _____

   The graphic designer felt it was important to include eye-catching contrast in the layouts. One way he achieved this was through the use of colour.

   (d) State two **other ways** in which the graphic designer has created contrast in the layouts.

   2

   _____

   _____

   _____

   The yellow and orange flash-bar behind the layout has been changed in layout 2 to create a style of balance that offers more visual impact.

   (e) State the style of balance achieved by the change.

   1

   _____

MARKS

1. **(continued)**

The red line in layout 2 is carefully chosen and positioned to enhance the layout.

(f) Describe one way in which the red line benefits layout 2 (do not repeat a previous answer).　　1

_____

_____

The web address and the 'World Electronics' text are placed in the spaces at the top and bottom of the layouts.

(g) State the names given to these spaces in a layout.　　2

Space at the top _____

Space at the bottom _____

(h) State the name of the DTP feature applied to the web address in layout 1.　　1

_____

Total marks　15

MARKS | DO NOT WRITE IN THIS MARGIN

2.   A furniture company wants to expand its range of desk lights and has employed a design engineer to create a new flat-pack version. The design engineer used 3D CAD to illustrate her proposal.

CAD ILLUSTRATION OF LAMP   **END ELEVATION**   **ELEVATION**   **PLAN**

The design engineer used the extrude command to make the base of the lamp. The base of the lamp requires two rectangular holes, identical in size and accurately centred on the base, to allow the vertical components to fit in.

An incomplete profile with one rectangle correctly in place is shown below.

SKETCH OF PART   **INCOMPLETE PROFILE**

(a)   Describe how the second hole can be drawn on the incomplete profile using only the information shown here. You may sketch directly onto the incomplete profile to help explain your answer.

2

_____

_____

_____

MARKS | DO NOT WRITE IN THIS MARGIN

2. (continued)

A range of CAD components are illustrated below.

(b) Describe, **using 3D CAD terms**, how you would assemble and constrain the components above. You may use sketches to illustrate your answer.   **4**

_____

_____

_____

_____

MARKS | DO NOT WRITE IN THIS MARGIN

2. **(continued)**

The bolt and the wing-nut were loaded from a 3D CAD library of standard components.

(c) Describe two benefits of a CAD library of standard components.   2

_____

_____

_____

30°

VIEW X

(d) Identify the type of pictorial view shown at view X.   1

_____

(e) Explain how view X can be used to support a customer.   1

_____

_____

MARKS DO NOT WRITE IN THIS MARGIN

2. (continued)

Two illustrated versions of the lamp are shown below.

The design engineer illustrated the 3D CAD model by applying different materials. This tested the appearance of the lamp in different materials and colours.

(f) Describe two other ways the 3D CAD model can be used to test the design of the lamp. 2

_____

_____

_____

Total marks 12

3. Images and orthographic production drawings of a new candle holder are shown opposite. It is being marketed as the OVO Candle Holder.

The OVO Candle Holder is a single component and has a second component, the mirror, added. It is not sold with the tea-light candle and the drawings below do **not** include a tea-light candle.

OVO
candle holder

MARKS | DO NOT WRITE IN THIS MARGIN

3.   (continued)

The view of section A–A is incomplete.

(a) Complete the view of section A–A by applying British Standards conventions and adding relevant features. You should sketch or draw the missing features directly onto the incomplete section A–A or you may annotate section A–A to describe your answer.

7

MARKS

3. **(continued)**

The orthographic production drawings are to be dimensioned to support manufacture.

(b) Add three dimensions, of the types listed below, to the orthographic views on the previous page.

Measure three suitable sizes on the drawings before adding the dimensions, correctly applying British Standards conventions, including scale.

- One length   2

- One breadth   2

- One diameter   2

The end elevation shown below is to have the mirror and tea-light candle added in an orthographic exploded view.

(d) Indicate suitable positions for the mirror and the tea-light candle in the exploded end elevation below. You may sketch or draw your answer or annotate the drawing to explain your answer.   2

EXPLODED END ELEVATION

Total marks 15

4. A company who specialise in scale model construction kits and wooden toys have produced two promotional adverts. The adverts will be used to promote the company to different target markets.

The first advert is aimed at a **target market** comprising:

Gender   Male and female
Age   8–12 years and their parents
Interests   Toys and creative play
TV influences Cartoons and children's programmes

The second advert focuses on a **target market** comprising:

Gender   Male
Age   35–65 years
Interests   Crafts and modelling
TV influences Home improvement shows

Advert 1

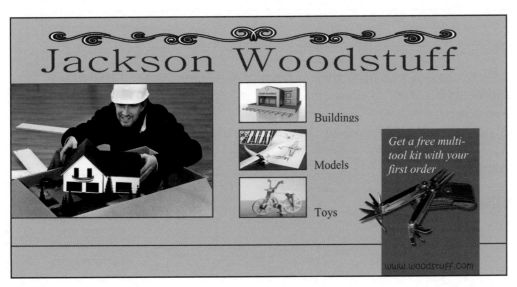

Advert 2

MARKS | DO NOT WRITE IN THIS MARGIN

4. (continued)

Advert 1 makes use of the colour red in the company name.

(a) State whether red is an advancing or a receding colour.   **1**

_____

(b) Describe the effect this colour has on the title in the layout of advert 1.   **1**

_____

_____

(c) Explain why the colours used in the layout of advert 2 were chosen.   **1**

_____

_____

The two adverts use very different font styles in the **company name**.

With reference to the font styles:

(d) Explain why the different fonts are considered suitable for each advert.

Advert 1: Font Style Kristen ITC   **1**

_____

_____

Advert 2: Font style Batang   **1**

_____

_____

The company chose not to print their promotional adverts. Instead, they sent them to potential customers using email.

(e) Describe one advantage and one disadvantage of this marketing approach.

Advantage _____   **1**

Disadvantage _____   **1**

Total marks   7

MARKS

5. A new set of headphones have been released by SND1.

To promote their new headphones, SND1 have employed a graphic designer to create a new display stand. The display stand will be made from sheet metal.

3D CAD illustrations and orthographic views of the design are shown below.

PLAN

ELEVATION   **END ELEVATION**   **ILLUSTRATED PICTORIAL VIEW**

The graphic designer chose to make a 3D CAD model rather than a full-size card prototype of the display stand.

(a) Give two reasons why a 3D CAD model was more suitable than the card prototype.   2

_____

_____

_____

The graphic designer gave the illustration to a CAD engineer, including key information about the display stand. One piece of information stated: **A/C 400mm**.

(b) Explain the term 'A/C' and how it is used to draw this product.   2

_____

_____

_____

5.   (continued)

The graphic designer initially only made the illustrated pictorial view of the stand. The CAD engineer created the orthographic views shown below.

ELEVATION   END ELEVATION

(c) Give two reasons why the CAD engineer would produce orthographic views of the display stand.

2

_____

_____

_____

_____

(d) Complete the end elevation shown above by plotting the edges on the surface generators. You may sketch or draw lines or plot corner points. Do not include hidden detail.

4

5.   (continued)

The graphic designer used 2D CAD software to generate the true shape of the sloping face of the hexagonal prism.

(e)   Identify the correct true shape by ticking a box below.   1

Total marks 11

[END OF MODEL PAPER]

Model Paper 3

Whilst this Model Paper has been specially commissioned by Hodder Gibson for use as practice for the National 5 exams, the key reference documents remain the SQA Specimen Paper 2013 and the SQA Past Papers 2014 and 2015.

National Qualifications
MODEL PAPER 3

Graphic Communication

Duration — 1 hour and 30 minutes

Total marks — 60

Attempt ALL questions.

All dimensions are in mm.

All technical sketches and drawings use third angle projection.

You may use rulers, compasses or trammels for measuring.

Use **blue** or **black** ink.

Before leaving the examination room you must give this booklet to the Invigilator.
If you do not, you may lose all the marks for this paper.

MARKS

1.

When you break through the pain barrier you need the drink to refresh your body, sooth the mind and ease your thirst

www.refreshsportsdrinks.co.uk

Final promotional layout for 'Refresh' isotonic sports drink

Colour Fill

Slogan

When you break through the pain barrier you need the drink to refresh your body, sooth the mind and ease your thirst

Jogger

Product name

Refresh

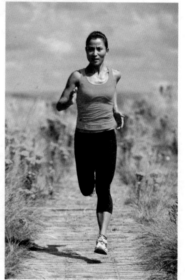

Original graphic items before editing for use in promotional layout

MARKS

1. **(continued)**

Shown at the top of the previous page is a promotional layout for a new soft drink called 'Refresh'. Some of the original graphic items used in the layout are shown at the bottom of the previous page.

Note: Do not refer to **resizing** in any of your answers and **do not repeat** your answers.

(a) State the name of the **DTP edit** used to prepare the **colour fill** for use in the final layout.

1

_____

(b) State the name of the **DTP edit** used to prepare the **slogan** for the final layout.

1

_____

(c) State the full name of the **DTP edit** used to prepare the **jogger** image for the final layout.

1

_____

(d) Describe how the DTP edit from part (c) **benefits** the layout.

1

_____

_____

(e) State the name of **one DTP edit** used to prepare the **product name** for use in the layout.

1

_____

The web address is located in the space at the bottom of the page.

(f) State what this space is called.

1

_____

Alignment has been used in the final promotional layout.

(g) State exactly **where** alignment is used in the final layout.

1

_____

MARKS | DO NOT WRITE IN THIS MARGIN

1.   (continued)

(h)   State how the use of alignment **benefits** the layout.   1

_____

_____

(i)   Describe **two** different ways in which the graphic designer has created **unity** in the layout.   2

_____

_____

_____

_____

(j)   Describe how the graphic designer has created **depth** in the layout.   1

_____

_____

(k)   Explain how the graphic designer has made the bottle the most **dominant** item in the layout.   1

_____

_____

The **colour matching** or **colour picker** tool (also called the eye-dropper tool) was used in the creation of the 'Refresh' layout.

(l)   Explain the benefit of this tool in creating the 'Refresh' layout.   1

_____

_____

Total marks 13

2. A product design engineer has sketched an idea for a simple egg cup and given this to a CAD technician for them to create a 3D CAD model.

The elevation and plan of the egg cup body, along with a sketch of the completed egg cup are shown below.

Ø50

Plan

45

Elevation

Pictorial View

The CAD technician used the **revolve** command to model the egg cup body.

(a) Describe, **using the correct dimensions and 3D CAD modelling terms**, how you would use 3D CAD software to model the egg cup body. You may use sketches to support your answer.   3

_____

_____

_____

MARKS | DO NOT WRITE IN THIS MARGIN

2. **(continued)**

A complete egg cup, a sectioned egg cup and the CAD modelling tree are shown below.

Egg cup

Sectioned egg cup

Modelling tree

PART	EGG_CUP		
FEATURE NAME		CONDITION
REVOLVE PROFILE		360
EXTRUDE PROFILE		5MM [GROUP I]
FILLET EDGES		RIOMM [GROUP I]
CIRCULAR ARRAY		ARRAY [GROUP I]
SHELL SOLID		WALL 2MM

UPDATE
END

The first egg cup model was rejected as the legs were hollowed, and this could allow food to become trapped if the egg cup was manufactured.

(b) State how this error could be corrected.   1

_____

Total marks   4

3. Production drawings for a new shelf unit, the 'GEO' shelf, are shown below.

PLAN

GEO shelf

ASSEMBLY DRAWING

NOT TO SCALE

Date: 14.9.13

Drawn by: B. Grant

ELEVATION

END ELEVATION

MARKS | DO NOT WRITE IN THIS MARGIN

3. **(continued)**

The drawings of the cylinder are to be dimensioned so that they can be manufactured.

Measure the orthographic drawings below.

(a) Dimension the views of the cylinder fully and to scale to enable manufacture.   **4**

Apply British Standards conventions correctly.   **4**

Other important features are missing from the drawings of the cylinder.

(b) Add the missing features to the views below. Apply British drawing standards correctly.   **1**

| CYLINDER DRAWING | CLIENT - GEO SHELVES | ALL SIZES IN mm | SCALE 1:2 | |

MARKS | DO NOT WRITE IN THIS MARGIN

3. (continued)

An exploded pictorial view of the shelf assembly is shown below.

(c) Explain how the clarity of this exploded view can be improved.   1

_____

The pictorial views of components show six designs for shelves and uprights.

Pictorial component views (a–f)

(a)   (b)   (c)   (d)

(e)   (f)

(d) State which two of the pictorial component views represent the shelf and the upright used in the 'GEO' shelf unit.

The **shelf** is pictorial component letter _____.   1

The **upright** is pictorial component letter _____.   1

MARKS

3.   (continued)

Pictorial assembly drawing

The **pictorial assembly drawing** shown above is a common type of pictorial view.

(e)   Identify the type of pictorial assembly drawing shown.   **1**

_____

The drawing, view X, shown on the opposite page, is incomplete.

(f)   Complete the drawing, view X, by adding the missing features and applying British Standards conventions. You may sketch or draw your answer directly onto view X or you may annotate the view to describe your answer. Do not include hidden detail.   **3**

(g)   Add the **correct** view title under the drawing, view X.   **1**

Total marks **17**

3.   (continued)

view X

A

A

ELEVATION

MARKS | DO NOT WRITE IN THIS MARGIN

4. An architect has chosen to begin a new project by sketching design proposals in a pictorial format. The architect will present these pictorial sketches to the client and discuss their needs.

The architect has created a 2-point perspective preliminary sketch to discuss with the client.

(a) Describe why this form of pictorial graphic is suitable for this purpose.   **1**

_____

_____

An architect is considering moving from manual drawing equipment to CAD.

The architect investigated the option and has chosen to stay with manual equipment rather than change to CAD.

(b) Describe two reasons why the architect may have chosen to stay with manual equipment.   **2**

_____

_____

_____

MARKS | DO NOT WRITE IN THIS MARGIN

4. **(continued)**

The architect will create a range of drawing types, including floor plans and site plans.

(c) State the scale most suitable to each plan.

Site Plan scale: _____ **1**

Floor Plan scale: _____ **1**

Total marks **5**

MARKS

5. An environmental charity wants to encourage people to recycle old batteries. They employed a design engineer to make a 'Battery Bin' where people could drop used batteries.

PLAN

END ELEVATION   **ELEVATION**

The graphic designer used 3D CAD to make a 3D model.

(a) Describe, **using 3D CAD modelling terms**, how the CAD model was created. You may use sketches to illustrate your answer.   4

_____

_____

_____

_____

5.   (continued)

2D CAD drawings will be produced to enable CNC manufacture. The 'Battery Bin' will be formed from sheet metal. A surface development is required to be marked onto the metal.

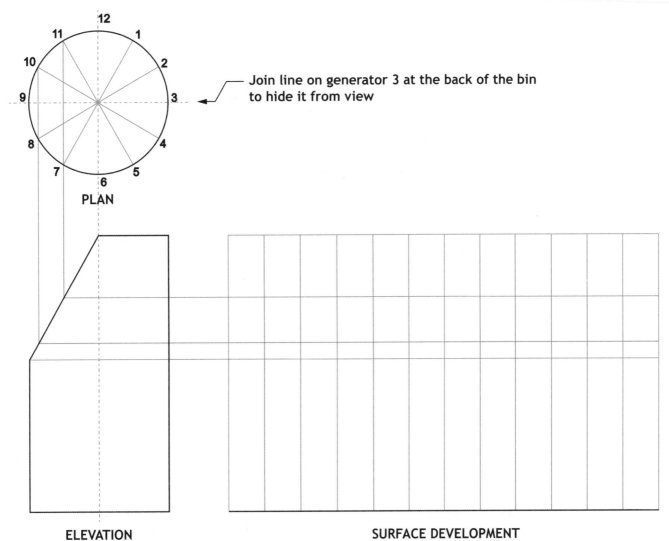

Join line on generator 3 at the back of the bin to hide it from view

PLAN

ELEVATION   SURFACE DEVELOPMENT

MARKS | DO NOT WRITE IN THIS MARGIN

(b) Complete the generators by adding numbers to the surface development.   1

(c) Complete the surface development by marking the sloping surface on the generators and adding the outlines. You may sketch your answer or mark crosses on the generators and annotate to describe your answer.   3

5.   (continued)

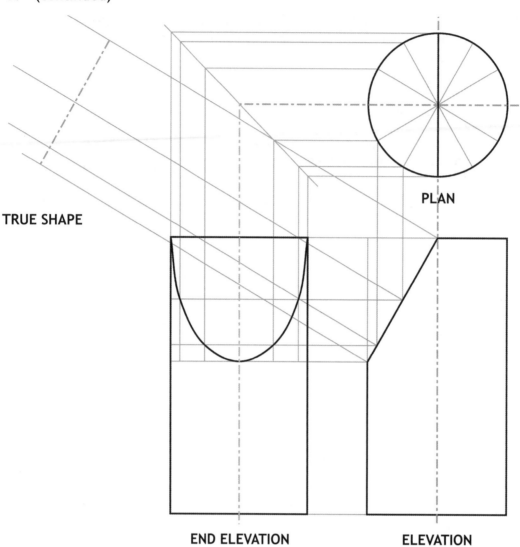

TRUE SHAPE

PLAN

END ELEVATION   ELEVATION

A graphic designer has been employed to design a graphic for the top of the 'Battery Bin'. The graphic designer has requested the **true shape** of the front of the bin.

MARKS

5.   (continued)

(d)   Identify the correct true shape by ticking a box below.   1

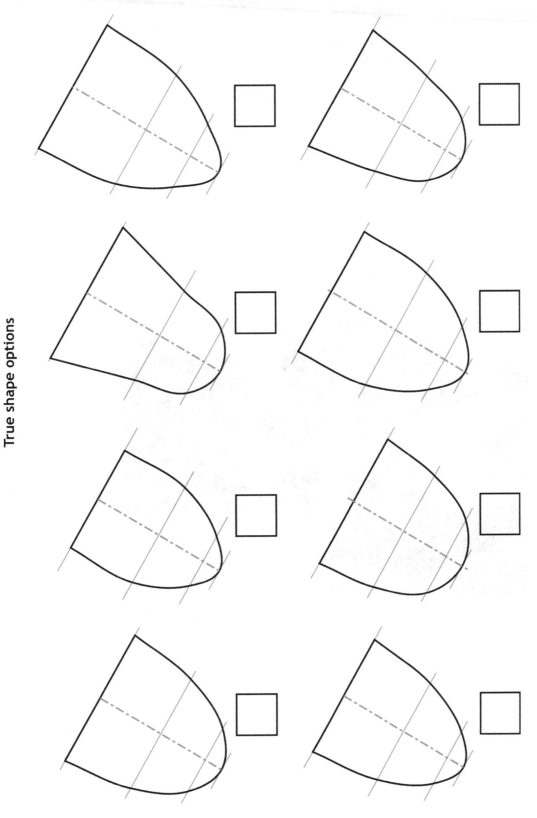

True shape options

Total marks   9

MARKS DO NOT WRITE IN THIS MARGIN

6. The following public information signs have all been used in an international airport where travellers are often in a hurry.

(a) State two reasons why graphic symbols, rather than textual information, are used in an international airport.

Reason 1 _____ **1**

_____

Reason 2 _____ **1**

_____

The colours chosen for the cafe seating area in the airport are mostly greens and neutral colours with some orange furniture providing the accent colour.

(b) Describe one way in which this colour scheme might benefit travellers. **1**

_____

_____

(c) Describe one way in which the colour scheme might support the identity of the airport. **1**

_____

_____

Total marks   **4**

MARKS | DO NOT WRITE IN THIS MARGIN

7. A takeaway company is launching a new range of healthier burgers.

A packaging designer made a preliminary sketch of half of the packaging, shown below. The packaging will be made from two identical hexagonal pyramids.

The company employed a CAD technician to create a 3D model of their new burger box. The first and final steps are shown below.

Preliminary sketch

Wall thickness 0.5mm

Inside Hexagon A/C 100mm

Plan

30°

40

Elevation

Final stage

First stage

(a) Describe, with reference to the **sizes in the preliminary sketch**, the modelling techniques used to model this half of the burger box. You may use sketches to illustrate your answer.   3

_____

_____

_____

MARKS | DO NOT WRITE IN THIS MARGIN

7.   (continued)

The CAD technician used 2D CAD to make the orthographic drawing and the surface development.

PLAN

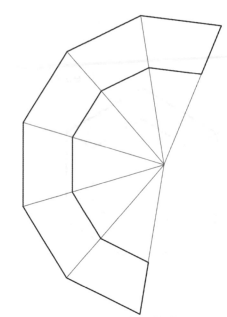

SURFACE DEVELOPMENT
FOR TOP OR BOTTOM

ELEVATION

END ELEVATION

True length is used to generate a surface development.

(b) Identify, on the drawing above, where the true length is measured from.   **1**

The surface development requires fold lines.

(c) Identify the correct line type for a fold by ticking a box below.   **1**

- - - - - - - - - - - - ☐   — - — - — - — - — - ☐

—— - — - — - —— ☐   · · · · · · · · · · · · · · ☐

·································· ☐   - - - - - - - - - - ☐

MARKS

7. (continued)

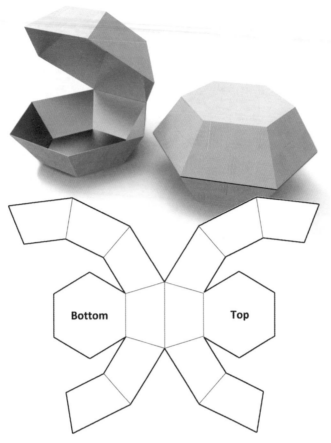

Surface development viewed from the outside of the packaging

Areas of textual information need to be added to the packaging, as indicated in the drawing below:

- Product name
- Sale-by-date
- Nutrition information

(d) Identify, on the surface development above, where the key information must go.

3

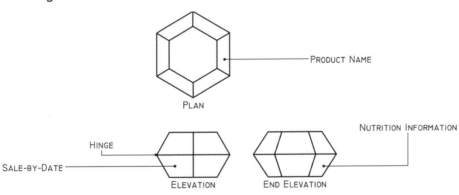

Total marks   8

[END OF MODEL PAPER]

NATIONAL 5

2014

N5

National Qualifications 2014

Mark

X735/75/01

Graphic Communication

THURSDAY, 8 MAY
1:00 PM – 2:30 PM

Fill in these boxes and read what is printed below.

Full name of centre

Town

Forename(s)

Surname

Number of seat

Date of birth
Day   Month   Year

D D M M Y Y

Scottish candidate number

Total marks — 60

Attempt ALL questions.

Write your answers clearly in the spaces provided in this booklet. Additional space for answers is provided at the end of this booklet. If you use this space you must clearly identify the question number you are attempting.

All dimensions are in mm.

All technical sketches and drawings use third angle projection.

You may use rulers, compasses or trammels for measuring.

Use **blue** or **black** ink.

Before leaving the examination room you must give this booklet to the Invigilator; if you do not, you may lose all the marks for this paper.

SQA

1. A graphic designer for a football magazine is commissioned to design a chart or graph. It should display the information in the table below in a visually stimulating and easy to read manner.

English Premier League players' average annual basic wages from 2000–2010	
Season	Average annual basic wage
2000–2001	£451,274
2001–2002	£566,932
2002–2003	£611,068
2003–2004	£651,222
2004–2005	£630,355
2005–2006	£685,748
2006–2007	£778,103
2007–2008	£960,377
2008–2009	£1,066,391
2009–2010	£1,162,350

(a) State the most suitable type of chart or graph to use when presenting the information in the table above.　　1

_____

(b) Explain **one** reason for using this type of chart or graph.　　1

_____

_____

Total marks　2

2. An advertising company has produced a promotional graphic to be used at a sports stadium. The graphic will be placed on the advertising boards around the pitch.

The initial layout is shown below.

Layout 1

(a) State **one** instance where **harmony** has been used in **layout 1**.

1

_____

_____

The graphic artist has decided to change the background colour to violet as shown below.

Layout 2

(b) (i) Explain a reason for changing the background colour to violet.

1

_____

_____

(ii) State whether violet is an advancing or receding colour.

1

_____

(iii) Describe the effect the violet background colour has on the watch.

1

_____

_____

MARKS | DO NOT WRITE IN THIS MARGIN

2. (continued)

The graphic artist wants to change the shade of violet used for the background colour as shown below.

Layout 3

(c) Explain how to create a **shade** of violet.   1

_____

_____

(d) Describe **two** examples of **unity** in **layout 3**.   2

Method 1 _____

_____

Method 2 _____

_____

(e) Describe how the desktop publishing technique '**bleed**' has been used in **layout 3**.   1

_____

_____

(f) Describe how the desktop publishing technique '**reverse**' has been used in **layout 3**.   1

_____

_____

MARKS

2. (continued)

The owners of the sports stadium decide to show the advert on their electronic advertising boards.

(g) State **two** environmental benefits of advertising this way.   2

Benefit 1 _____

Benefit 2 _____

Total marks 11

[Turn over

3. Two stages in the production of a 3D CAD model of a headphone connector are shown below.

Stage 1

Before   After

Stage 2

Before   After

(a) State the name of the 3D modelling feature which has been used in Stage 1.

1

_____

(b) State the name of the 3D modelling feature which has been used in Stage 2.

1

_____

Total marks   2

4. Two building symbols which are commonly found in sectional views of buildings are shown below.

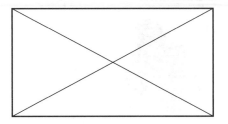

Symbol 1   **Symbol 2**

State the name of: 2

Symbol 1 _____

Symbol 2 _____

5. A 3D CAD model of a new craft knife design is shown below.

State **three** disadvantages to a design company of using 3D CAD modelling instead of traditional manual modelling.   3

1 _____

2 _____

3 _____

MARKS | DO NOT WRITE IN THIS MARGIN

6. A variety of views of a child's wooden toy train are shown below.

Diagram 1a:

Plan

Diagram 1b:
Component 1
Main body

Component 2
Lower body

Component 3
Wheels
and axle

Elevation

End Elevation

Symbol X

(a) State the name of the type of drawing shown in Diagram 1a.   1

_____

(b) State the name of Symbol X in Diagram 1a.   1

_____

(c) Describe the purpose of Symbol X.   1

_____

6. (continued)

Four potential Sectional Elevations of the toy train views are shown below.

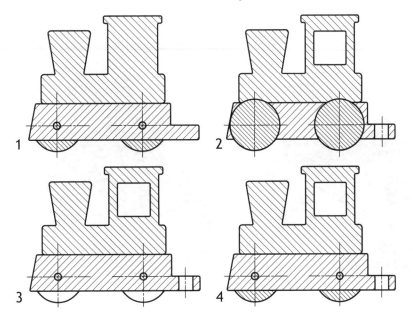

Diagram 2: Sectional Elevations on A—A

(d) State, with reference to Diagram 1a and Diagram 2, the correct Sectional Elevation on A—A.

1

Four potential Sectional End Elevations of the toy train views are shown below

Diagram 3: Sectional End Elevations on B—B

(e) State, with reference to Diagram 1a and Diagram 3, the correct Sectional End Elevation on B—B.

1

MARKS | DO NOT WRITE IN THIS MARGIN

6. **(continued)**

Two pictorial views of the toy train are shown below.

View 1   **View 2**

(f) State the name of the pictorial view shown at:

    (i) View 1   1

_____

    (ii) View 2   1

_____

(g) State the name of another **two** types of pictorial views which would be suitable to show the train.   2

Pictorial type 1

_____

Pictorial type 2

_____

MARKS | DO NOT WRITE IN THIS MARGIN

6. (continued)

A partial End Elevation complete with relevant dimensions (Diagram 4a) of the toy train is shown below. An End Elevation of the train track is shown (Diagram 4b).

Diagram 4a: Dimensioned Partial End Elevation of the toy train

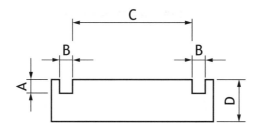

Track End Elevation

Diagram 4b: End Elevation of train track

(h) State, with reference to Diagram 4a and 4b, a dimension for:

(i) **A** _____   1

(ii) **B** _____   1

(iii) **C** _____   1

(iv) **D** _____   1

[Turn over

MARKS | DO NOT WRITE IN THIS MARGIN

6.   (continued)

The train track can be made up with the four different track tiles shown in Diagram 5.

Tile Type A   Tile Type B   Tile Type C   Tile Type D

Diagram 5: Example Track Tiles

Diagram 6 shows a completed track layout using a minimum number of tiles.

Number of type A tiles: [0]

Number of type B tiles: [0]

Number of type C tiles: [1]

Number of type D tiles: [3]

START   END

Diagram 6: Completed Track Layout

MARKS | DO NOT WRITE IN THIS MARGIN

6.   (continued)

Three incomplete track designs are shown below.

(i)   State, with reference to Diagrams 5 and 6, the minimum number of each type of track tile required for each track design. All open ends must be blocked off.

Tiles may be rotated.

(i)   Track design 1:   4

Number of type A tiles: ☐

Number of type B tiles: ☐

Number of type C tiles: ☐

Number of type D tiles: ☐

(ii)   Track design 2:   4

Number of type A tiles: ☐

Number of type B tiles: ☐

Number of type C tiles: ☐

Number of type D tiles: ☐

(iii)   Track design 3 (your track must reach both END points):   4

Number of type A tiles: ☐

Number of type B tiles: ☐

Number of type C tiles: ☐

Number of type D tiles: ☐

Total marks 25

7. A door handle and door plate were designed using 3D modelling software.

An exploded isometric view of the door handle and door plate is shown below.

Door plate

Door handle

A preliminary orthographic sketch of the door handle (not to scale) is shown below.

60

40

10

135

PLAN

15

Ø20

□10

30

ELEVATION

MARKS

7. (continued)

A Ø20 circle is sketched before the extrude command is used to create step 1.

(a) State the length of the extrusion used in step 1.

Step 1

1

_____

(b) Describe, with reference to correct dimensions and 3D CAD modelling terms, how you would complete step 2 and step 3.

Step 2

Step 3

You may use sketches to support your answer.

4

[Turn over

7. **(continued)**

The door plate is needed to secure the handle to the door. The production orthographic drawing (not to scale) for the door plate is shown below.

End Elevation   Elevation

(c) Describe, with reference to correct dimensions and 3D CAD modelling terms, how you would create the door plate.

You may use sketches to support your answer.   3

MARKS | DO NOT WRITE IN THIS MARGIN

7.   (continued)

In order to manufacture the door plate, the back of the plate is hollowed out as shown below.

(d)   State the name of the 3D modelling technique used to hollow the door plate.

1

_____

(e)   State **three** advantages of computer aided drawing over manual drawing methods.

3

Advantage 1 _____

Advantage 2 _____

Advantage 3 _____

When producing the door plate the CAD command 'zoom' is used.

(f)   State one way in which the 'zoom' command would be useful.

1

_____

_____

Total marks   13

[Turn over for Question 8 on *Page eighteen*

MARKS | DO NOT WRITE IN THIS MARGIN

8. Two graphic items A and B are shown below.

(a) Indicate, using a tick (✓), if
     Graphic Item **A** is:

     1

     Preliminary   ☐

     Promotional   ☐

     Production   ☐

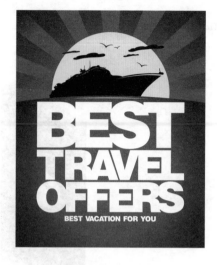

Graphic Item **A**

(b) Indicate, using a tick (✓), if
     Graphic Item **B** is:

     1

     Preliminary   ☐

     Promotional   ☐

     Production   ☐

Graphic Item **B**

Total marks   2

[END OF QUESTION PAPER]

MARKS

ADDITIONAL SPACE FOR ANSWERS

MARKS | DO NOT WRITE IN THIS MARGIN

ADDITIONAL SPACE FOR ANSWERS

N5

National
Qualifications
2015

Mark

X735/75/01

Graphic Communication

THURSDAY, 30 APRIL
1:00 PM – 2:30 PM

Fill in these boxes and read what is printed below.

Full name of centre

Town

Forename(s)

Surname

Number of seat

Date of birth

Day	Month	Year	Scottish candidate number

Total marks — 60

Attempt ALL questions.

All dimensions are in mm.

All technical sketches and drawings use third angle projection.

You may use rulers, compasses or trammels for measuring.

Write your answers clearly in the spaces provided in this booklet. Additional space for answers is provided at the end of this booklet. If you use this space you must clearly identify the question number you are attempting.

Use **blue** or **black** ink.

Before leaving the examination room you must give this booklet to the Invigilator; if you do not, you may lose all the marks for this paper.

[BLANK PAGE]

DO NOT WRITE ON THIS PAGE

MARKS | DO NOT WRITE IN THIS MARGIN

1. "Birdy" is a new type of bird box produced by Bio, an environmentally conscious retailer. The lid and body are made from sheet metal. A CAD technician produced the rendered 3D CAD illustration and the pictorial line drawing shown below.

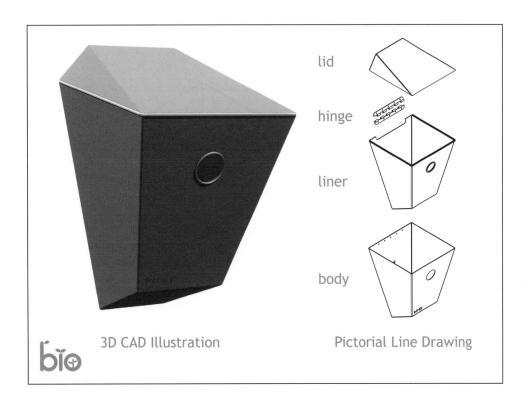

3D CAD Illustration   Pictorial Line Drawing

(a) State **two** reasons why the CAD technician would have produced the rendered 3D CAD illustration shown above.   2

_____

_____

_____

(b) State the type of pictorial line drawing shown above.   1

_____

(c) Describe **one** advantage that the pictorial line drawing has over the 3D CAD illustration.   1

_____

_____

[Turn over

MARKS | DO NOT WRITE IN THIS MARGIN

1. (continued)

The CAD technician initially created the 3D CAD illustration of the bird box. In preparing for manufacture the CAD technician has been asked to create the orthographic views shown below.

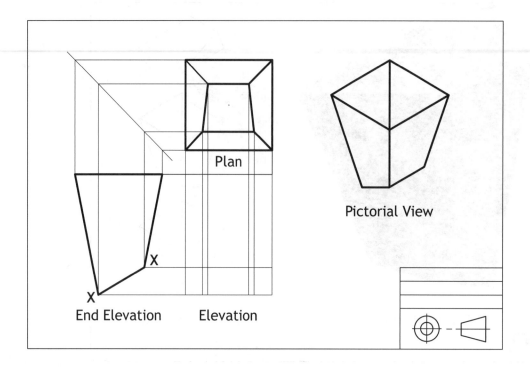

Plan

Pictorial View

End Elevation   Elevation

(d) Identify the correct elevation by ticking a box below, ignore wall thickness.

1

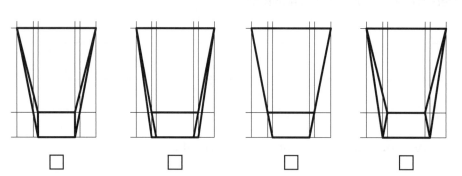

☐   ☐   ☐   ☐

(e) State **two** pieces of information you would find in a title block other than the 3rd angle projection symbol shown above.

2

_____

_____

MARKS | DO NOT WRITE IN THIS MARGIN

1. **(continued)**

To assist in the manufacture of the body of the bird box, the CAD technician was asked to generate the true shape of sloping face X - X.

(f) Indicate using a tick (✓) the correct true shape. Use a ruler or trammel to measure.   1

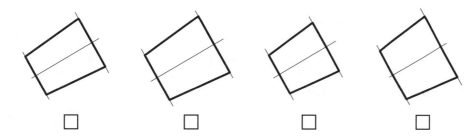

☐   ☐   ☐   ☐

To complete the 2D CAD drawings required for manufacture, the CAD technician has been asked to identify the placement of key features.

(g) Indicate on the sketch of the preliminary surface development below where the hole and hinge will be positioned.

Use "A" to indicate the hinge and "B" to indicate the entrance hole.   2

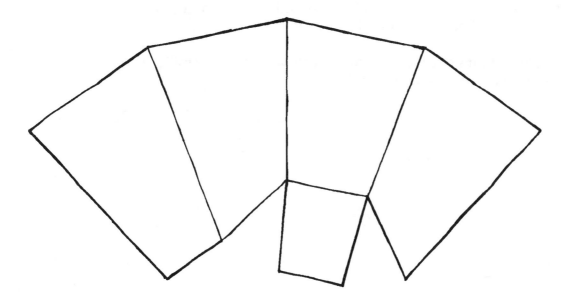

Preliminary sketch of the surface development

[Turn over

MARKS | DO NOT WRITE IN THIS MARGIN

1.   (continued)

Three line types that will be used to complete the 2D CAD drawings to British Standards Conventions are shown below.

(h)   State the uses of the following line types:

(i)   A continuous thick line.

_____

1

_____

(ii)   A chain thin double dashed line.

_____

1

_____

(iii)   A chain thin line.

_____

1

_____

Prior to manufacture the CAD technician was asked to produce layouts for cutting the lid and body out of a single sheet of metal.

(i)   Explain, in terms of environmental impact, why careful consideration of the layout of multiple parts is important.

1

_____

_____

MARKS | DO NOT WRITE IN THIS MARGIN

1.   (continued)

A graphic designer was asked to create a 'point of sale' graphic that will be used in Bio's retail outlets to promote the bird box. The graphic designer was asked to communicate the environmental qualities of the brand. The finished graphic is shown below.

(j)   Describe **two** ways that the designer has graphically communicated the environmental qualities of the brand.

2

_____

_____

_____

_____

_____

_____

[Turn over

MARKS

2. "Module" is a shelving system consisting of two sizes of shelves and connecting hubs that can be arranged in a variety of ways. Rendered 3D CAD illustrations are shown below.

300 shelf

connecting hub

600 shelf

Rendered 3D CAD illustrations

An orthographic sketch of the connecting hub is shown below.

End Elevation   Elevation

MARKS | DO NOT WRITE IN THIS MARGIN

2.   (continued)

(a) Describe, using the correct dimensions and 3D CAD modelling terms, how you would use 3D CAD software to model the hub. You may use sketches to support your answer.

6

MARKS | DO NOT WRITE IN THIS MARGIN

2.   (continued)

Orthographic assembly drawings of an arrangement of the shelving system are shown below.

300 shelf

600 shelf

End Elevation   Elevation

(b) Indicate using a tick (✓) the **two** pictorial assembly drawings that match the arrangement shown in the orthographic assembly drawing above.   **2**

MARKS | DO NOT WRITE IN THIS MARGIN

2. **(continued)**

The CAD technician produced a variety of arrangements of the shelving system.

(c) State the CAD feature that would allow the CAD technician to produce a variety of assemblies quickly and efficiently.   1

_____

[Turn over

MARKS | DO NOT WRITE IN THIS MARGIN

3. "Toob" is a self assembly chair produced by FORM UK. The chair has been designed for ease of assembly using a **matching system**. Tubes with shaped hollow cores connect to corner brackets with matching pegs. Rendered 3D CAD illustrations of the assembled chair and a detail view showing the **matching system** are shown below.

detail showing peg and
core matching system

assembled chair

An exploded view, orthographic drawings and details of the matching system used for the three different lengths of tube that form the frame are shown on the **supplementary sheet for Question 3**.

A graphic designer has been tasked with constructing a parts list for the assembly instructions. An incomplete parts list is shown below.

(a) Indicate in the table below, the quantity of each type of corner bracket required and the shape of pegs that will be used for each.

Bracket 2 has been completed for you.   6

	matching system	angle	Quantity
Bracket 1	/	90°	
Bracket 2	△ / □	20°	2
Bracket 3	/	106°	
Bracket 4	/	90°	

MARKS | DO NOT WRITE IN THIS MARGIN

3. (continued)

Illustrated views of the 20° connecting bracket and a tube are shown below. There are three stages in the assembly of these components.

(b) Indicate by **shading** the relevant **surfaces** and state using 3D CAD terms how you would assemble and constrain the components shown above.

Stage one has been shaded for you.   **5**

Stage 1

Stage 2

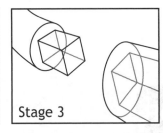

Stage 3

Constraint used   Constraint used   Constraint used

_____   _____   _____

[Turn over

MARKS | DO NOT WRITE IN THIS MARGIN

3.   (continued)

FORM UK have decided to launch the new chair at a number of international furniture trade shows. During the shows, promotional materials for the new chair will be distributed.

The designer was tasked with producing a postcard which met the following design specification:

> The postcard must:
>
> o Create impact.
>
> o Encourage further exploration of the product.
>
> o Provide basic details of function.
>
> o Appeal to a target audience of 18-40 year old males and females.
>
> o Create a modern layout.
>
> o Create a sense of depth.

The final design is shown below.

Front of postcard   Back of postcard

FORM UK are happy that the above postcard meets all of the specification points.

(c) Describe how the postcard has met the specification points.   4

_____

_____

_____

_____

_____

_____

MARKS | DO NOT WRITE IN THIS MARGIN

3. (continued)

FORM UK commissioned the graphic designer to also develop a mobile app to launch the chair. The graphic designer was tasked with creating a layout that used similar graphic content to the postcard. An image of the finished app is shown below.

(d) Describe **two** advantages that an electronic promotional item gives the company over traditional promotional items.

2

_____

_____

_____

_____

(e) Explain how the production of the app can be simplified by having the graphic elements already digitally produced.

2

_____

_____

_____

_____

4. An extreme sports company, Equilibrium, have designed a new skateboard.

A CAD technician was provided with orthographic preliminary sketches of the wheel component.

ELEVATION   END ELEVATION

MARKS | DO NOT WRITE IN THIS MARGIN

4.   **(continued)**

   (a)   Describe, with reference to correct dimensions and 3D CAD modelling terms, how you would use 3D CAD software to model the wheel.

   You may use sketches to support your answer.

   3

[Turn over

MARKS

4.   (continued)

Equilibrium employed a graphic designer to produce point of sale displays for retail outlets. The point of sale includes a scaled up version of the skateboard used as a stand, holding four skateboards with graphics applied to it.

The designer produced two different ideas for use on the point of sale unit, shown on the **supplementary sheet for Question 4.**

MARKS | DO NOT WRITE IN THIS MARGIN

4. **(continued)**

Equilibrium requested the graphic designer produce ideas that make use of alignment.

(b) Describe how the graphic designer has used the design principle of **alignment** in **both** of the ideas shown on the **supplementary sheet for Question 4**.　　　4

Idea 1

_____

_____

_____

_____

Idea 2

_____

_____

_____

_____

(c) Describe how the graphic designer has used the following design principles in idea 1.

　(i)　Contrast　　　1

　　_____

　　_____

　(ii)　Unity　　　1

　　_____

　　_____

[Turn over

MARKS | DO NOT WRITE IN THIS MARGIN

4. (continued)

The design for the point of sale is to be printed on expensive glossy vinyl by an external printing company. The graphic designer produced a scaled down test print on A3 paper before sending to the external printing company.

(d) Describe **two** reasons why the graphic designer would do this.

2

4. **(continued)**

An exploded isometric and the working drawing of the bracket used to hold the skateboards to the display board are shown below.

EXPLODED ISOMETRIC

PLAN

SECTIONAL END ELEVATION
A-A

ELEVATION

The CAD technician recognised **five** pieces of information in the working drawing that did not adhere to British Standard conventions.

(e) State the **five** errors found in the drawing.

You may annotate the drawing to support your answer.

5

_____

_____

_____

_____

_____

[END OF QUESTION PAPER]

MARKS | DO NOT WRITE IN THIS MARGIN

ADDITIONAL SPACE FOR ANSWERS

MARKS | DO NOT WRITE IN THIS MARGIN

ADDITIONAL SPACE FOR ANSWERS

[BLANK PAGE]

DO NOT WRITE ON THIS PAGE

National Qualifications 2015

X735/75/11

Graphic Communication
Supplementary Sheet

THURSDAY, 30 APRIL

1:00 PM – 2:30 PM

Supplementary Sheet for use with Questions 3 and 4.

Supplementary Sheet for use with Question 3.

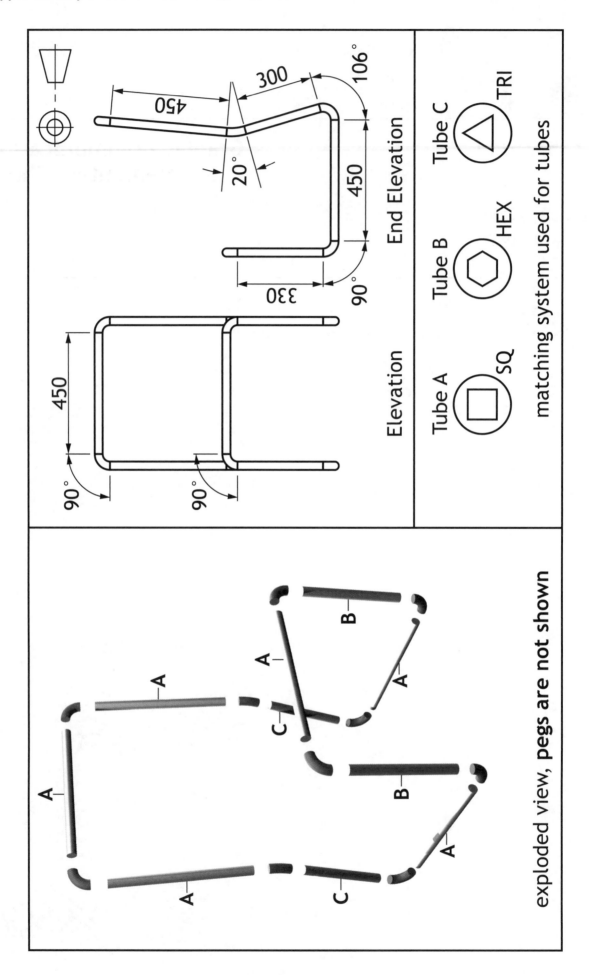

End Elevation

450

300

106°

20°

90°

330

450

Elevation

450

90°

90°

Tube A   SQ

Tube B   HEX

Tube C   TRI

matching system used for tubes

exploded view, pegs are not shown

Supplementary Sheet for use with Question 4.

Idea 1

Idea 2

[BLANK PAGE]

DO NOT WRITE ON THIS PAGE

NATIONAL 5 | ANSWER SECTION

1. (a) Background colours are receding or contrasting and help the red advancing colour to stand out. **1**

(b) Text wrap; wrap text **1**

(c) To separate items; to help create structure; to emphasise the company name **1**

(d) Flow text; flow text along a path **1**

(e) Reverse; reverse text (*'Font style' will not be accepted as an answer.*) **1**

(f) Creates contrast with the straight lines in the layout; creates a close connection between the product and the slogan; reflects the sentiment of the text: soft and smooth, suggests comfort or cushioning, suggests movement. **1**

(g) Graded, gradient or gradiation fill **1**

2. (a)

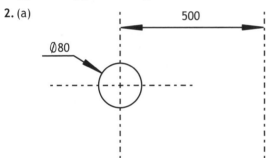

Draw a circle of DIA80mm *(1 mark)*, 500mm away from a centre line. *(1 mark)*

Revolve the circular profile 180° round the centre line. *(1 mark)* **3**

(b) Select the flat face of a slot; draw a mirror line; select a plane. *(1 mark for either of these)* Use the mirror command to mirror the component. **2**

(c)

Constraining the back to the arm

Constraining the seat to the arm

Mating the three faces of the seat and back

Constraining the opposite arm

Assemble the chair seat and back requiring three mates. *(1 mark)* Mate the chair to leg/arm base. *(1 mark)* Mate the chair to leg/arm back. *(1 mark)* Constrain opposite arm using same technique. *(1 mark)* **4**

3. (a) and (b)

ISOMETRIC VIEW

Plastic Fixing Clip
All sizes in mm
Not to scale
Plastic location Clip

SECTION A-A · ELEVATION

2

Table of British Standards errors and omissions in the fixing clip production drawing	
Your numbered error or omission	Description of error or omission
1	This should be a centre line, not a solid line.
2	The number is underneath the dimension line; it should be on top
3	This dimension should be a diameter, not a radius.
4	Cross-hatching is in the wrong direction; one component = one direction
5	Units should not be shown; they appear already in the title block.
6	Centre line is missing.
7	The web is section and should not be.
8	Open arrows on the dimension line; these should be closed.
9	The plan is upside-down.

8

(c) **CAD models** are electronic and can be quickly and easily sent to China via email attachments. **1**

Drawing standards are common around the world and can be understood by all users. Drawing standards help overcome language barriers. **1**

(d) CAD models are easily modified to take account of changes to the design; CAD models can be tested before being manufactured; the CAD model can be used to produce a CNC prototype; CAD models can be rendered to produce a realistic image; CAD models can be tested in computer simulations; production drawings can be easily generated from CAD models. **2**

(e) Exploded pictorial view iii **1**

4. (a) The pale blue colours used in the improved sign are suitable because they are associated with cleanliness and are calming in nature; the two tones used help the user follow the information across the sign. (*Or any other suitable answer*) **2**

(b) The sans-serif font used has no formatting (italic, bold, underline) and is clear and easy to read.
OR
The new font is simpler and more modern. It is less formal, less old-fashioned, etc. It is not italicised. (*There is no need to specifically mention serif or sans-serif typefaces.*) **1**

(c) The line separating 'Department' and 'Floor' is removed; the department titles are accurately aligned; the floor numbers are 'reduced' on the improved sign; departments are grouped; 'You are here' is clear on the improved sign; the coloured banding makes connecting the department and floor easier. (*Any two points, for one mark each*) **2**

5. (a) Isometric exploded view A **1**

(b) When the physical hook assembles, the hook will need to be placed on top of the wall bracket from the top. **1**

(c)

VIEW A **VIEW B**
1

(d) Section A–A is view S. **1**

(e) Section B–B is view Y. **1**

(f) Exploded views show how the components in a product fit together; exploded views can help to show the assembler or consumer the best way to assemble a product. **1**

(g) Sectional views give an understanding of how parts fit together; sectional views can show the features inside components and assemblies that cannot normally be seen. **1**

(h) Webs; shafts; spindles; axles; nuts and bolts. (*Any one*) **1**

(i) An assembly drawing is a drawing of a product that has more than one part and the parts are put together as they will be in the real product. Component drawings are drawings of individual parts. **1**

(j) Component drawings are dimensioned prior to manufacture because each part is normally manufactured separately and assembled later. Dimensioning assembly drawings would be confusing because it may not be clear which component the dimensions apply to. **1**

6. (a) Line graph
OR
Bar graph **1**

(b) The line graph has a time base and is the best choice to show a flow or trend over a period of time.
OR
The bar graph will give a comparison between sales in different months. **1**

(c) A table **1**

(d) The data is too complex to present using any of the other types of information graphic. **1**

7. (a) North arrow; scale of drawing; room names; dimensions; ceiling lights; electrical sockets; wall switches. (*Any three*) **3**

(b) ▬▬▬██████████████████▬▬▬

(*Symbol added in a suitable position to any room.*)

8. (a) Matching the colour of green in two items; the red flashbar is layered behind the title and the young people and the student ID card which physically connects them all; the phone number is in very close proximity to the image of young people. (*Any one*) **1**

(b) By layering items on top of other items; ID card over flashbar; young people over the flashbar; etc. (*Any one*) **1**

(c) Alignment occurs between the title and the ID card; the right end of the title and the right edge of the phone number are aligned; the flow text is carefully aligned to the ID card. (*Any one*) **1**

(d) Depth by layering (near and far); size (big and small text, people, etc.); vertical and horizontal; straight and curved (wavy). (*Any one*) **1**

(e) Contrast can make the layout eye-catching. This is important to attract attention or when the poster is moving along a roadside and has a brief viewing time. **1**

(f) The most dominant item is: group of young people OR the title OR the ID card.
The designer created dominance by: the image of young people is on the top layer, at the front, they are in close up (large) OR title is on a red (advancing) background and so stands out well OR ID card is layered on top of the title and the curved shape gives it dominance. (*Any one pair*) **1**

NATIONAL 5 GRAPHIC COMMUNICATION MODEL PAPER 2

1. (a)

	DTP edit
The L-COM product name	rotate/flip
The slogan ('A NEW DAWN ...' etc.)	flow text along a path
The body text	left aligned or text wrap
The image of the L-COM product	drop shadow

4

(b) Layering and overlapping images on top of other images creates a physical connection; using an accent colour (red or blue) in more than one area creates a unity through colour; text wrap creates a connection between the body text and the product. *(Any two)* **2**

(c) The product is pictorial and creates a strong 3D image; the product is in perspective and has a near corner and a far corner; the product is on the top layer; the drop shadow creates depth and emphasis. *(Any two)* **2**

(d) Vertical colour fill and horizontal line; near and far; 2D shapes and a 3D image; large and small text. *(Any two)* **2**

(e) Asymmetric balance **1**

(f) It creates depth by passing behind the product image; it helps create asymmetric balance; it creates contrast with the blue colour fill; it creates unity with the red button; it creates strong alignment with the header and footer. *(Any one)* **1**

(g) Space at the top   <u>Header space</u>
Space at the bottom   <u>Footer space</u> **2**

(h) Reverse text *('Reverse' will be accepted)* **1**

2. (a) Draw a construction line horizontally through the incomplete profile. (In the middle – 60 mm from top and bottom). *(1 mark)*
Select the rectangular slot and use the mirror tool to mirror the rectangle about the centre. *(1 mark)* **2**

(b)

Centre axis to the upright, nut and bolt to the base. Mate the flat face of upright to inside of base (A to A as shown above).
Mate the flat face of bolt to outside of base (B to B as shown above).
Mate the flat face of the nut to outside of base (C to C as shown above). **4**

(c) Standard components are pre-drawn and can be assembled directly – this saves time. They are drawn to the particular standards of common component parts and can be modified as the design develops and changes. **2**

(d) Exploded isometric view. **1**

(e) Customers can see easily see how the lamp assembles; customers do not need to understand complex orthographic drawings; customers may find it easier to follow a drawing rather than a written description. *(Any one)* **1**

(f) The lighting effect can be simulated; the range of motion can be tested; the strength of materials can be tested. *(Any two)* **2**

3. (a)

(b) **One length:** Any suitable length with BS correctly applied *(1)* and the size correctly scaled *(1)*.
One breadth: Any suitable breadth with BS correctly applied *(1)* and the size correctly scaled *(1)*.
One diameter: Any suitable diameter with BS correctly applied *(1)* and the size correctly scaled *(1)*.
(No marks awarded for dimensioning height.)　　**6**

(d) *(One mark each for showing or describing the tea-light candle and mirror in 2D and exploded in line with their locations.)*

EXPLODED END ELEVATION

　　2

4. (a) Advancing colour　　**1**

(b) It makes the title stand out more; it throws it forward; it creates contrast with the other main colours in the layout. *(Any one)*　　**1**

(c) The (neutral brown) colours should appeal to the older target market; the browns suggest natural materials; the colours represent wood craft (the hobby of the customer); the colours give the advert a more traditional look which is suitable for an older target market. *(Any one)*　　**1**

(d) **Advert 1:** The font is a fun style that will appeal to young children and their young parents; it supports (matches) the fun theme promoted through the toys. *(Any one)*　　**1**
Advert 2: The font is a more traditional, formal or old fashioned style that will appeal to the older target market (do not need to mention serif/sans-serif font); the font is more formal and likely to appeal to an older target market which likes traditional crafts. *(Any one)*　　**1**

(e) **Advantage:** It reduces paper costs; it is environmentally friendly (no paper production); it creates a more personal or direct contact with potential customers; it is immediate (quick) and can happen whenever the company likes without waiting for a magazine to come out. *(Any one or any other suitable answer)*　　**1**
Disadvantage: It may limit mass contact with potential customers; it may impact on the employment opportunities in paper publishing and production; it will require a large database. *(Any one or any other suitable answer)*　　**1**

5. (a) It is quicker/easier to modify a CAD model; CAD models can be used to create a surface development; CAD models can be illustrated to look like metal; CAD models can be illustrated in a range of scenes; it is easier to store a CAD file than a physical model. *(Any two)*　　**2**

(b) A/C means 'across corners'. It refers to the size of the hexagon on the display stand.　　**2**

(c) To aid manufacture; to aid production drawings with sizes; to add dimensions; to aid the DTP for the true shape on top; to understand the proportions of the stand from each elevation. *(Any two)*　　**2**

(d)

PLAN

ELEVATION　　　　END ELEVATION

　　4

(e)

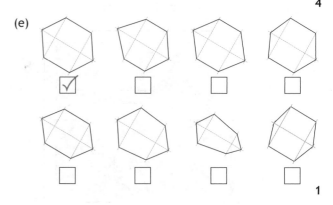

　　1

NATIONAL 5 GRAPHIC COMMUNICATION MODEL PAPER 3

1. (a) Transparency   1

   (b) Text wrap   1

   (c) Fully cropped
      OR
      Fully masked   1

   (d) It allows a new background to be introduced; allows layering; creates a shape to contrast with rectangles; emphasises the figure; allows the old background to be removed. *(Any one)*   1

   (e) Font style; reverse
      OR
      Font colour; drop shadow. *(Any one)*   1

   (f) Footer space   1

   (g) The product name, the slogan and the web address are all carefully aligned down the left hand edge.   1

   (h) Alignment helps bring a neatness, structure or organised look to the layout.   1

   (i) The colour fill (flashbar) connects the background, the product, product name and the jogger; the blue line connects the product and the figure; the text wrap connects the slogan to the figure; the red colour matching connects the product with the colour fill; blue is used in the background, the jogger and the line, connecting them visually; overlapping (layering) physically connects items that touch. *(Any two)*   2

   (j) Layering and overlapping images create depth; drop shadows behind the jogger and product name create depth. *(Any one)*   1

   (k) The bottle is larger in scale than other items; is on the top layer; is positioned close to a (rule of thirds) focal point. *(Any one)*   1

   (l) The colour of the bottle was selected with the colour picker and the colour fill was created in exactly the same colour.   1

2. (a)

Draw an ellipse with a major axis of 90 mm and minor axis of 50 mm. Trim the ellipse to leave ¼.	Revolve the profile 360°.	Select the top face and shell the solid to 2 mm.

                                          3

   (b) The shell solid command is in the wrong position in the modelling tree. Move it to just after the revolve profile.   1

3. (a) Marks awarded for showing or describing the four vital (scaled up) dimensions *(for 1 mark each). (Apply a 1mm tolerance throughout.)* Vital dimensions added without being scaled *(2 marks only)*. Each dimension must be described or shown **correctly** to British Standards *(for 1 mark each)*.
      (Dimension layout and style may differ from marking scheme but must conform to British Standards.)   4

   (b) *(Three centre lines correctly applied or described. All three required for 1 mark.)*   1

   (c) The components are not separated enough; create clear space between each component in the exploded view.   1

   (d) The **shelf** is pictorial component letter _d_.   1
      The **upright** is pictorial component letter _b_.   1

   (e) Oblique view   1

   (f) *(Cross hatching added or described and with direction changes and staggering. 1 mark for each section.)*   3

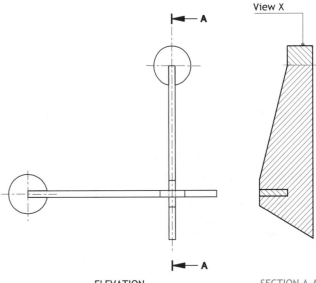

   (g) 'Section A–A' as shown above.   1

4. (a) Perspective graphics are more realistic and show proportion, with items further away getting smaller; a perspective drawing is easily understood by people without a technical background. *(Any one)*   1

   (b) The cost of retraining may be large; the high cost of purchasing CAD equipment and software; manual drawing equipment is already available. *(Any two)*   2

   (c) Site plan <u>1:200</u>   1
      Floor plan <u>1:50</u>   1

5. (a) Draw a circle on the base workplane and extrude as a cylinder.
Draw a subtracting shape on the frontal workplane and subtract it to make the slope.
Make the cylinder hollow by using the shell command.
Extrude a circular sketch on the sloping face to make a hole. **4**

(b) and (c)

JOIN LINE AT BACK OF BIN TO HIDE IT FROM VIEW

1 and 3

(d)

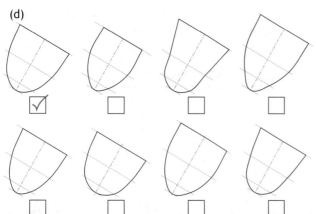

1

6. (a) **Reason 1:** Symbols overcome language barriers. **1**
Reason 2: Symbols are quicker to interpret than text. **1**

(b) Orange creates a refreshing contrast with green; green is a fresh and natural colour, both of which are important in a cafe or restaurant *(would also accept that orange is an appetite colour)*; green is a relaxing colour, important in a hectic airport. *(Any one)* **1**

(c) A common colour scheme creates a unified identity or impression; orange creates contrast with green and is, in this instance, a unifying accent colour. *(Any one)* **1**

7. (a) Extrude the hexagon 40 mm with a taper angle of 30°. Shell the solid 0.5 mm. **3**

(b)

PLAN

ELEVATION   END ELEVATION

True Length

SURFACE DEVELOPMENT FOR TOP OR BOTTOM **1**

(c)

1

(d)

Nutrition information

Product name

Bottom   Top

Sell-by-date

Surface development viewed from the outside of the packaging

3

NATIONAL 5 GRAPHIC COMMUNICATION 2014

1. (a) Line graph is the most suitable

(b) • Shows the steady growth over a specific period of time
 • Shows trend easily
 • No large differences between items on the "y" axis

2. (a) Green background and yellow watch

(b) (i) • Violet/purple looks more classy and luxurious
 • To create contrast with the yellow watch
 • To create contrast
 • To make the watch more eye catching

 (ii) Receding

 (iii) • Emphasises the yellow watch
 • Makes the yellow watch stand out more
 • To make the watch more eye catching

(c) Add black or grey

(d) • Yellow text 'UTZ' and yellow watch (or any yellow feature of the watch)
 • White circles/bubbles and white divisions on the watch face and white text.
 • Shape of watch face, bubbles and full stops.

(e) The watch/image/graphic runs into the margin space and/or off the edge of the advert

 Image overlaps the side/edge of the advert/page.

(f) • White text on violet background
 • Text changed to white

(g) • No printing so less ink/toner
 • No printing paper
 • No transportation as advert can be emailed to the stadium.

3. (a) Revolution/Revolved solid/Revolve

(b) Extrusion/Extrude

4. Symbol 1 – Sawn Timber
 Symbol 2 – Concrete

5. • Start-up costs
 • Staff training on new software/ technology
 • Cost to regularly update software
 • Costs for maintenance of equipment
 • Potential loss of work/files through system crashes
 • Easy theft of data/hacking
 • Ergonomic testing cannot take place

6. (a) Orthographic

(b) Third angle projection/Third angle

(c) • To show the way the views are projected/laid out
 • To show projection type used
 • Orientation/layout of views

(d) View 3

(e) View 6

(f) (i) Isometric view

 (ii) 2 point perspective view

(g) Oblique/1 point perspective/ planometric

(h) (i) 7.5mm

 (ii) 5mm

 (iii) 44mm

 (iv) Response must be larger than 7.5mm

(i) Some answers will have two combinations see below:

 (i) tileA= 0   0
   tileB= 0 or 0
   tileC= 2   4
   tileD= 3   1

 (ii) tileA= 0
   tileB= 0
   tileC= 1
   tileD= 2

 (iii) tileA= 1   1
   tileB= 1 or 1
   tileC= 4   3
   tileD= 1   2

7. (a) 40mm

(b) **Step 2**
 • On one end of the cylinder sketch/draw a rectangle 135mm × 30mm
 • Extrude the rectangle 10mm

 Step 3
 • On the other end of the cylinder sketch/draw a 10mm × 10mm square in the centre
 • Extrude the square 60mm

 Or any similar and appropriate process

(c) • Sketch a rectangle 120mm × 60mm and extrude 10mm
 • In the centre of the rectangle draw a circle Ø20mm and extrude subtraction/subtract 5mm.
 • In the centre of the circle above, sketch a circle Ø15mm and extrude as a subtraction/subtract 5mm

 Or any similar and appropriate process

(d) Shell

(e) Any of;
 • Library of common parts can be used to reduce time
 • Ease of editing
 • Ease of creating new designs from existing designs
 • Less physical storage space required
 • Portable files easier and quicker to transfer by digital means.
 • Accuracy
 • Ability to use in different scenarios (use as base for 3D models)
 • Used for simulations
 • Simultaneous working

(f) • Zoom allows the user to focus in on smaller details
 • to get an enlarged view of a small part

8. (a) Promotional

(b) Production

NATIONAL 5 GRAPHIC COMMUNICATION 2015

1. (a) Any two from:
- The graphic can be used for promotional/marketing reasons
- The graphic can aid discussions with the client prior to manufacture
- This type of graphic is more universally understood
- This type of graphic is more easily understood by non-technical people
- Provides a realistic representation of the product

(b) Exploded isometric view.

(c) Any one from:
- This type of graphic is more **informative** than the 3D CAD illustration
- It lets the viewer see how the product is assembled
- It lets the viewer see all the component parts of the product.

(d)

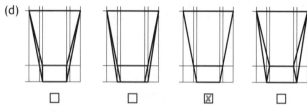

☐   ☐   ☒   ☐

(e) Any two from:
- Project title/title
- Name/name of draughtsperson/designer/approver
- Start date/completion date/print date/date
- Scale
- Drawing number/sheet number
- Dimensional tolerances
- Dimensional units used
- Document/drawing type

(f)

☐   ☐   ☒   ☐

(g)

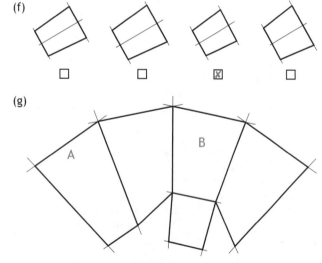

Sketch of the surface development

(h) (i) Visible outlines and edges

(ii) Bend Lines/Fold Lines

(iii) Centre Lines

(i) Any answer which details a reduction of waste materials or environmental concerns.

(j) Any two from:
- Use of natural textures such as the grass
- Green colour scheme is instantly recognisable with eco products
- Colour green is recognisable as being linked to nature, outdoors and similar connotations
- Brown 'natural' background/Printed on brown 'natural' coloured paper
- Logo directly references nature/natural environment (leaves)
- Amount of ink used has been kept to a minimum (lots of white space/line drawing uses less)

2. (a)
- Create initial profile making reference to correct dimensions 1
- Extrude profile 40 mm 1
- Fillet edges 20 mm front and back 1
- Create new sketch on any one of the three flat ends (circle DIA 20 mm) 1
- Extrude circle 40 mm 1
- Repeat last stage on the two remaining flat ends 1

(b)

☐   ☐   ☒

☐   ☒   ☐

(c) CAD Library

3. (a)

angle	matching system	angle	Quantity
Bracket 1	☐ / ☐	90°	2
Bracket 2	△ / ☐	20°	2
Bracket 3	△ / ☐	106°	2
Bracket 4	⬡ / ☐	90°	4

Answers for 1 & 4 may be reversed

(b)

Stage 1   Stage 2   Stage 3

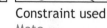

Constraint used   Constraint used   Constraint used
Mate   Mate   Mate

_____   _____   _____

(c) Any four from:
- Create impact — Bold/Bright/Vivid orange colour, contrasting colours (accept black & white), contrast of graphics to background; items 'stand out'; reverse, use of bold text.
- Encourage further exploration of the product — minimal information provided to entice consumers; silhouette graphics of chair do not give a complete picture/understanding of the product. Website/URL is provided.
- Provide basic details of function — abstract graphics of the 'matching system' (triangle, square and hexagon) and pictorial view of corner bracket hint at the products function. Text on back of postcard gives information on function.
- Appeal to a target audience of 18–40 year old males and females, font styles, non-gender specific colour choice and simple graphics appeal to both genders and age group. None of the graphic elements mentioned above exclude any section of the target market based on gender or age.
- Create a modern feel to the layout — background and graphics bleed to edges, minimal/simple overall style, use of white space, unconventional layout.
- Create a sense of depth — overlapping elements (text and graphics)

(d) Any two from:
- Is capable of reaching a larger target audience
- Post production editing is possible
- The electronic item can be adapted or expanded at a later date
- Can impart more information about the product to the viewer
- Hyperlinks to other aspects of the company can be included
- Ability to interact with the electronic promotional item
- No printing costs
- No waste of printing materials
- Flexibility to send/share in a number of ways
- Transport costs.

(e) Any two from:
- Graphic elements such as the logo, chair silhouette and shapes can be stored centrally and reused.
- Graphic elements can be dragged and dropped if the programs used are compatible.
- Having the elements already created saves time and effort.
- Font matching is easier
- Colour matching is easier
- Editing is possible of pre-existing graphics

4. (a) Revolve Technique;
- Create 2D sketch of profile   1
- Correctly dimensioned gap between profile and centre axis   1
- Revolve sketch 360 degrees around centre axis   1

(b) **Idea One**

Any of:
- Silhouettes are aligned centrally (vertically)
- The letter E of 'Equilibrium' aligns with top of the body of text
- Any reference to the white line running down the board with regard to alignment also acceptable
- Wheels of skateboard are aligned with the 'i' letters
- White circles centrally aligned

Idea Two

Any of:
- Body text and website have been **centrally** aligned with each other
- Lack of alignment creates "movement" on the graphic, reflecting the nature of the product
- Wheels of skateboard are aligned with the 'i' letters

(c) (i) • (White) line & circles
- Image against the orange background
- Black logo with orange background
- White against orange background
- Black text/image against white images
- Text directions
- Text styles

(ii) Any one from:
- White line running down the board ties elements together
- Use of line running down centre of board and line running through Equilibrium
- Repetition of (white) circles creates unity
- Black title and black text/image
- Images are all white

(d) Any two from:
- Allows designer to check for any errors/mistakes before final print
- Designer can show layout to client before final print
- Scaled down version uses less ink/toner/paper
- Can be printed quickly on a desktop printer — no need for specialist output equipment

(e) • Plan view is upside down/projected in 1st angle
- No letter labels on cutting plane
- Value of 75 on elevation is on wrong side of dimension line
- Missing centre lines on sectional end elevation
- Web has been sectioned
- Inconsistent hidden detail lines
- Leader lines touching
- Cutting plane missing thick ends
- Wrong line type used for centre lines on 3rd angle projection symbol
- Inconsistent application of 3rd angle projection

Acknowledgements

Permission has been sought from all relevant copyright holders and Hodder Gibson is grateful for the use of the following:

Image © Ting Hoo/Getty Images/Thinkstock (Model Paper 1 page 2);
Image © adam smigielski/Getty Images/iStockphoto/Thinkstock (Model Paper 1 page 2);
Image © bagiuiani — Fotolia (Model Paper 1 page 15);
Image © bagiuiani — Fotolia (Model Paper 1 page 15);
Image © d_arts/Shutterstock.com (Model Paper 1 page 15);
Image © Getty Images/iStockphoto/Thinkstock (Model Paper 1 page 16);
Image © eteimaging — Fotolia (Model Paper 1 page 17);
Image © Edyta Pawlowska/www.123rf.com/photo_15623110 (Model Paper 1 page 17);
Image © Ozerina Anna/Shutterstock.com (Model Paper 2 page 2);
Image © Gouraud Studio — Fotolia (Model Paper 2 page 11);
Image © Gouraud Studio — Fotolia (Model Paper 2 page 11);
Image © Tatyana Gladskih — Fotolia (Model Paper 2 page 11);
Image © smuki — Fotolia (Model Paper 2 page 11);
Image © Harvepino/Shutterstock.com (Model Paper 2 page 11);
Image © aleksangel — Fotolia (Model Paper 2 page 11);
Image © Chlorophylle — Fotolia (Model Paper 2 page 11);
Image © viperagp — Fotolia (Model Paper 2 page 11);
Image © shooarts — Fotolia (Model Paper 2 page 11);
Image © chamillew — Fotolia (Model Paper 2 page 11);
Image © Stanislav Dobrochaso — Fotolia (Model Paper 2 page 11);
Image © Olga Khoroshunova — Fotolia (Model Paper 3 page 2);
Image © Edie Layland — Fotolia (Model Paper 3 page 2);
Image © Philip Date/Shutterstock.com (Model Paper 3 page 2);
Image © Image © yewkeo/iStockphoto/Thinkstock (Model Paper 3 page 12);
Image © Image © antikainen/iStockphoto/Thinkstock (Model Paper 3 page 12);
Image © nahariyani100 — Fotolia (Model Paper 3 page 12);
Image © sjhaytov/iStockphoto/Thinkstock (Model Paper 3 page 18);
Image © haveseen — Fotolia (Model Paper 3 page 18);
Image © Dmitry Kutlayev/iStockphoto/Thinkstock (Model Paper 3 page 18);
Image © Kenishirotie/iStockphoto/Thinkstock (Model Paper 3 page 18);
Image © Nikolay Okhitin/Hemera/Thinkstock (Model Paper 3 page 18);
Image © AlexRoz/Shutterstock.com (2014 pages 3 & 4);
Image © Lena Pan/Shutterstock.com (2014 page 18);
Image © vector photo video/Shutterstock.com (2014 page 18).

Hodder Gibson would like to thank SQA for use of any past exam questions that may have been used in model papers, whether amended or in original form.